WONDERS OF THE HUMAN BODY

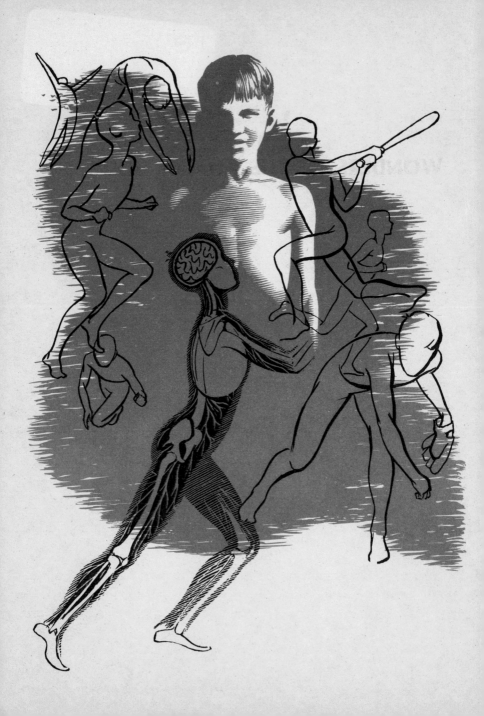

WONDERS

OF THE **HUMAN BODY**

WRITTEN AND ILLUSTRATED BY

ANTHONY RAVIELLI

SCHOLASTIC **BOOK SERVICES**

Published by Scholastic Book Services, a division
of Scholastic Magazines, Inc., New York, N.Y.

ALSO BY ANTHONY RAVIELLI

An Adventure in Geometry

Copyright 1954 by Anthony Ravielli. This edition is published by Scholastic Book Services, a division of Scholastic Magazines, Inc., by arrangement with The Viking Press, Inc.

5th printing . . . . . . November 1966

Printed in the U.S.A.

To My Mother and Father

ACKNOWLEDGMENTS

Many thanks to Harold Schwartz, editor of juvenile magazines, Parents Institute, for his invaluable assistance in the preparation of the manuscript; and to Dr. Joseph Sperling for his patience and cooperation.

CONTENTS

PART II. THE MUSCLES

PART III. THE BRAIN AND THE NERVOUS SYSTEM

PART IV. FUELING THE BODY

FOREWORD

Did you ever wonder why we look the way we do and do the things we do, such as walk and run and see and feel?

Your body is a machine that does many, many things. To do these things, it needs many, many parts. All these parts together are what we are. No one part is more important than another: the bones, the muscles, the vital organs are all members of a team working together.

Let us look at each part separately and see what it does.

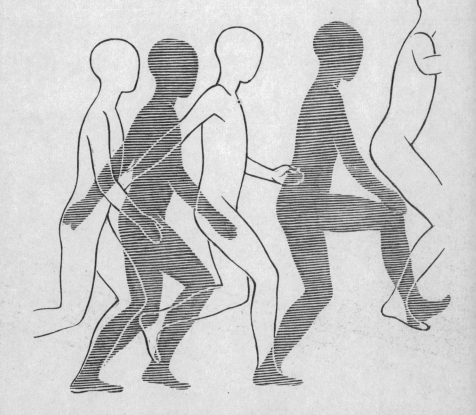

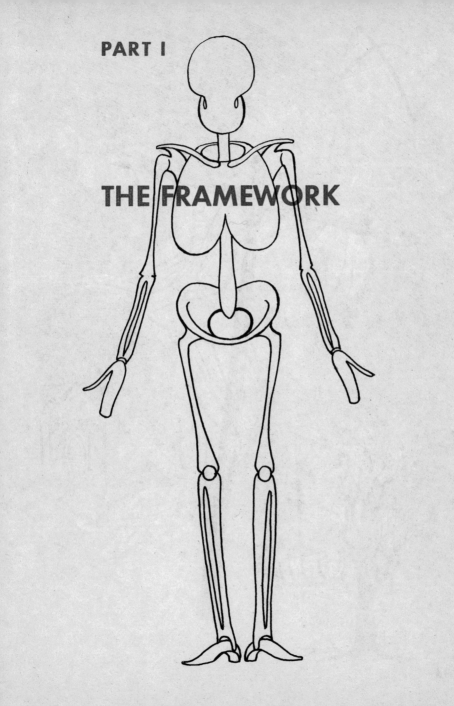

PART I

THE FRAMEWORK

THE FRAMEWORK

When we build a house, or make a kite or even a scarecrow, we need a framework. Without it the house would fall down, the kite would not fly, the scarecrow would be but a pile of rags. In each case it is the framework that supports the structure and gives it its shape.

So it is with us. Without a framework we would be shapeless and unable to move. The framework not only supports us; it also protects our vital organs. The framework is made of bone and is called the skeleton.

It takes approximately 200 magnificently designed bones to make the human skeleton. The question is, what do they look like and how do they work?

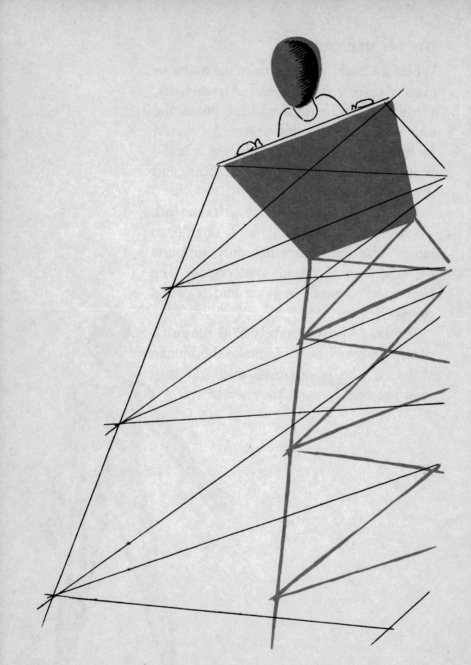

LET US START AT THE TOP...

THE SKULL

A MILLSTONE IS EITHER OF A PAIR OF CIRCULAR
STONES BETWEEN WHICH GRAIN IS GROUND

The 22 bones of the head are divided into two groups: the cranium, and the bones of the face, which include the bone of the lower jaw. All of them combined are called the skull. The cranium, made up of 8 bones, is the big hollow ball that forms the shape of the head. But unlike a ball, the cranium has a little opening at the bottom, the use of which is explained later in the book.

Below the cranium are the 14 bones of the face. They are irregular in shape, and attached to them are the muscles of the face. The two hollows that are the sockets for your eyes are formed by the bones that make your cheeks. The passages for the nose and ears, the grooves into which fit the teeth, and the teeth themselves, are all in the area we describe as the face. The bones of the face, with the exception of the lower jaw, are firmly joined to the cranium. They do not move.

The lower jaw is the only part of the head that moves. Shaped like a horseshoe, it is hinged to the base of the cranium. This makes it possible to open and close the mouth, a very important action. Without it you would not be able to eat, talk or sing.

When you chew, the teeth in the lower jaw rise to meet the upper teeth, giving the mouth the action of millstones.

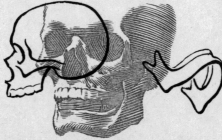

YOUR SPINE IS VERY MUCH LIKE

A STRING OF SPOOLS

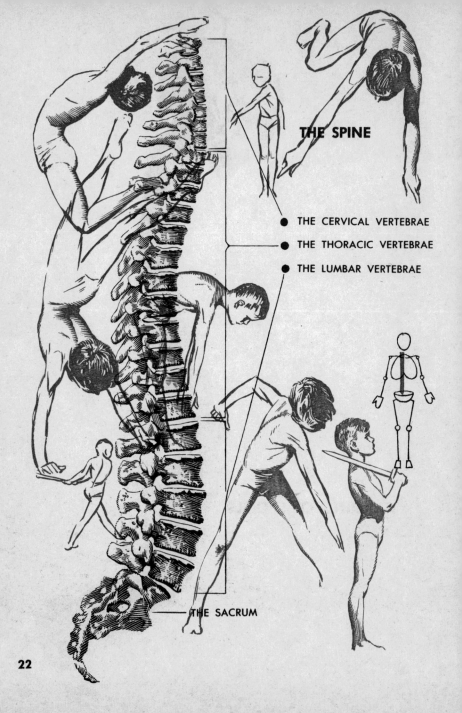

THE SPINE

- THE CERVICAL VERTEBRAE
- THE THORACIC VERTEBRAE
- THE LUMBAR VERTEBRAE

THE SACRUM

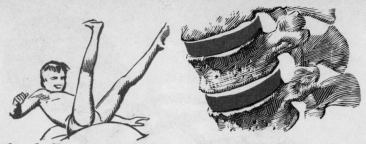

The skull rests on a column of 24 "spools" set one upon the other. Each "spool," or section, is called a vertebra, and the column is the spine. The spine holds you straight and erect, yet you can still turn your head, twist your body, and bend forward and backward. Each vertebra is rigid and is made of solid bone, but the string of vertebrae, like a string of beads, can assume many shapes.

The spine is perfectly balanced and is so ordered in its arrangement that it forms the most beautiful line in the body. Each vertebra is separated by a little cushion, which also makes the spine a shock absorber. Any tremendous impact at the base of the spine is absorbed along the way by each separating cushion, and is not felt by the time it reaches the top of the spine. If it were not for this, you would jar your brain with every step you took.

The spine does a big job for you. It does more than support the entire upper part of the body. The top 7 vertebrae in the spine are called the cervical vertebrae and are the most flexible. They allow the head to turn in all directions. The ribs spring from the following 12, which are called the thoracic vertebrae. The lumbar vertebrae are the last 5; they allow you to bend forward and backward. The sacrum below the last vertebra is immovable and is wedged between the bones of the hips.

ATTACH WIRE RINGS

TO THE SPOOLS...THESE ARE
YOUR **RIBS**

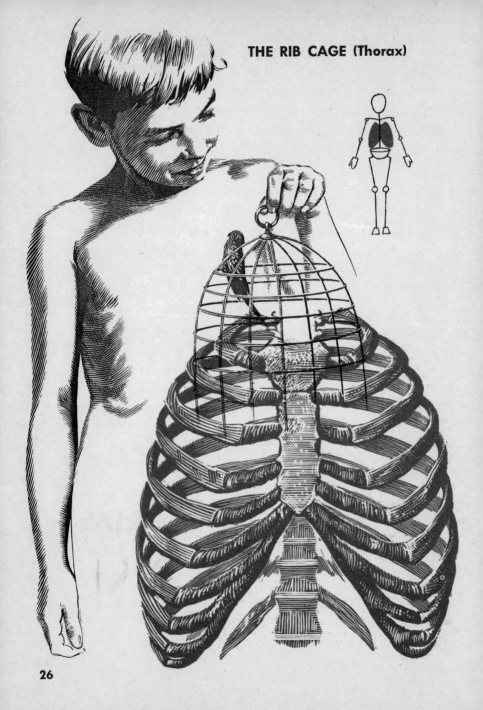

THE RIB CAGE (Thorax)

The thorax is like a bird cage with an opening at the top and no bottom. Fastened to the 12 thoracic vertebrae, on each side, are oval-shaped strips of bone called ribs. They form the house that protects your lungs and are the bones that give the chest its shape.

The ribs start at the spine and all but two—the floating ribs—are attached to the sternum, or breastbone. The breastbone is a short flat bone shaped like a small dagger pointing down. It runs from the root of the neck down the front side of the chest for 5 or 6 inches.

The connection of the ribs to the breastbone is made with an elastic tissue called cartilage. The rib cartilage extends from the breastbone very much as branches extend from a tree. Because of the flexible cartilage and the loose attachment of the ribs to the spine, the rib cage can expand, raise, and lower. This makes it possible for you to breathe.

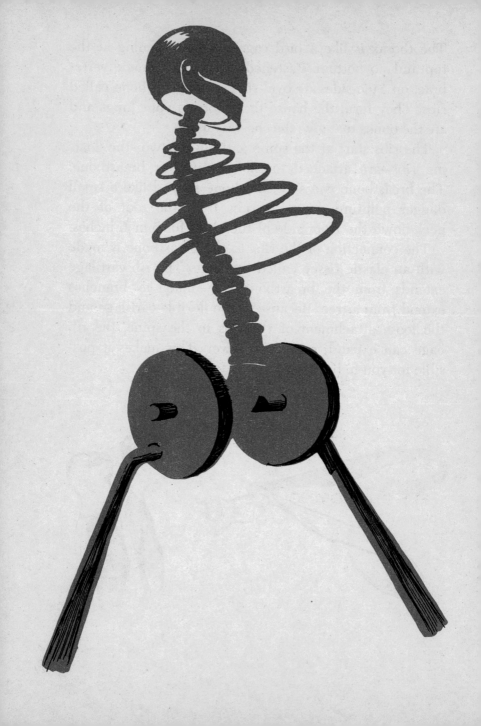

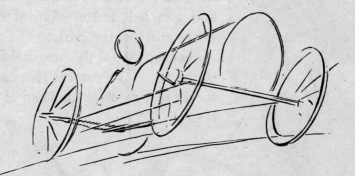

LET'S GET MOVING —

THE HIP BONES (Pelvis)

The immovable bones of the hips form a bony ring, and support the entire upper body. They are the axle on which the legs revolve.

The hips consist of 2 bones which flare outward and are shaped like the wings of a butterfly. Curved and wide at the top, these bones turn in toward the center to form a cuplike shape, with a large opening at the bottom of the cup. The part of the hips on which you hang your trousers and gun belt is the edge of the flaring bones at its widest part.

On each side of the hips, below the flare of the bone, is a cavity. This cavity is the socket that receives the head of the thighbone.

THE THIGHBONE (Femur)

The strongest and heaviest bone of all the 206 bones you have in your body is the thighbone, or femur. It starts at the hip and ends with the knee. It is similar to a walking stick and even looks like one. This walking stick has a short neck that is bent inward at a slight angle. At the end of the neck is a ball that fits into the socket of the hip, allowing the lower limb to move in all directions so that you can run, jump, kick, and dance.

So efficient is this ball-and-socket joint that no matter what position you assume the thigh will still support its share of the burden. These 2 mighty thighbones are the sturdy pillars on which your body rests.

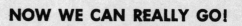

NOW WE CAN REALLY GO!

THE BONES OF THE LEG

The lower limb is a spoke that turns in all directions and bends at the knee. The section above the knee is, as you know, the thighbone. From the knee down to the ankle are the 2 bones of the leg: the shinbone and the calfbone. The strong shinbone (tibia) and its neighbor, the frail calfbone (fibula), run parallel to each other. Though they are equal in length, the shinbone alone makes the joint at the knee. The calfbone is attached to the under surface of the wide head of the shinbone. At the lower end both bones hang free to form the ankle.

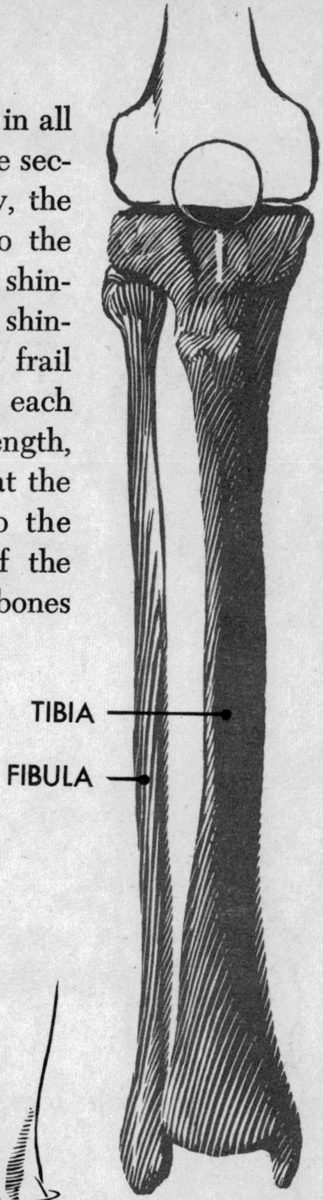

TIBIA

FIBULA

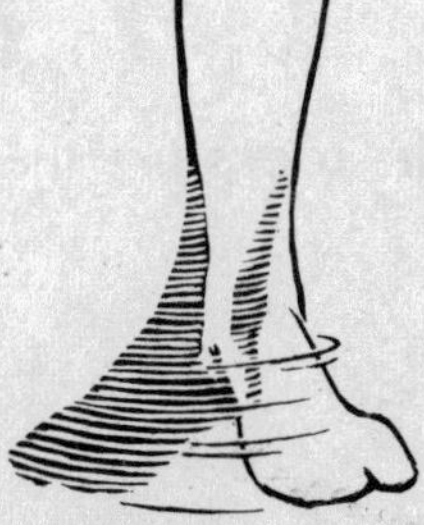

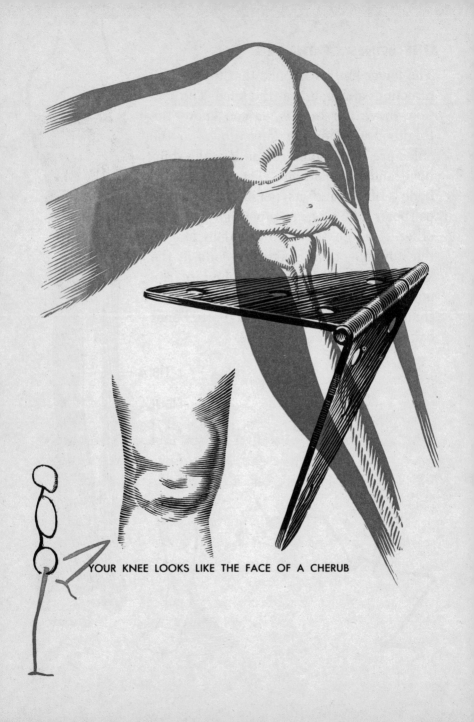

YOUR KNEE LOOKS LIKE THE FACE OF A CHERUB

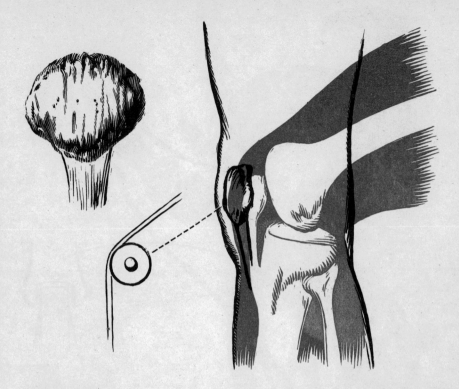

THE KNEE

The hinged joint we call the knee makes the motion of the leg smooth and easy. This joint allows the leg to bend in only one direction and locks when the leg is straight. In front of the knee joint is the kneecap— a loose bone the size and shape of a chestnut. It protects the knee and helps it to bend smoothly. The kneecap is attached to the tibia by a ligament, which is a band of very tough tissue. The ligament, although flexible, is not elastic and cannot stretch. This allows a bone to which it is attached free movement without dislocation.

THE FOOT AND ANKLE

The foot supports all your weight, and a great deal more.

The secret of the foot's strength lies in its peculiar structure: its 26 bones are set in a semicircle, forming a perfect arch. Engineers have used the principle of the arch in building bridges, but the arch was in the human foot a long, long time before bridges were built. The body makes use of many mechanical principles. A good example is the way the foot hangs suspended at the ankle.

Wedged in between the shinbone and the calfbone, the foot can move up and down like a seesaw, can point its toes in or out, and place its sole against the sole of the other foot. Arched for support, the foot is hinged at the ankle for motion.

The motion of the foot is aided by flexible toes, which, like fingers, can move and wiggle and clutch. The foot makes walking easy and graceful.

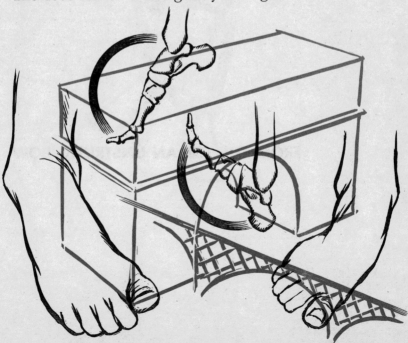

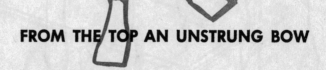

FROM THE TOP AN UNSTRUNG BOW

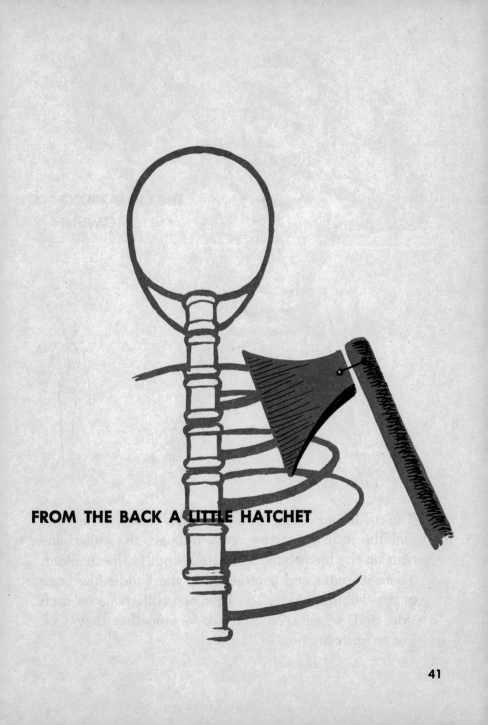

FROM THE BACK A LITTLE HATCHET

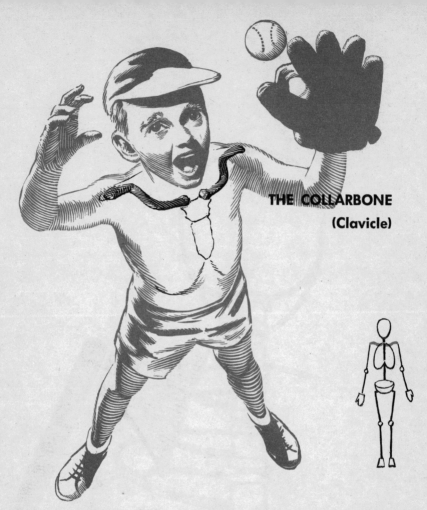

THE COLLARBONE

(Clavicle)

The collarbone is the connecting link between the body and the arm. A narrow, curved bone, the collarbone rests on the breastbone and extends out to the shoulder. There its outer end is attached to the handle-like bone in the shoulder blade. You have one collarbone on each side, and, when seen from above, together they look like an unstrung bow.

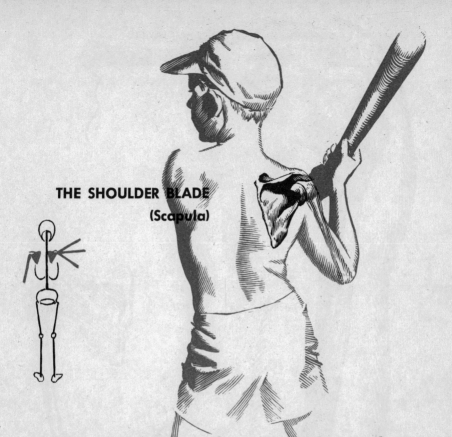

THE SHOULDER BLADE
(Scapula)

The shoulder blade is a flat, triangular bone with a handle-like bone rising from it. The shoulder blades are in the upper part of the back of the chest. They are not connected to the ribs, but slide over them. In the outer point of the triangular shoulder blade, there is a socket. The ball at the top end of the bone of the upper arm (the humerus) fits into this socket.

43

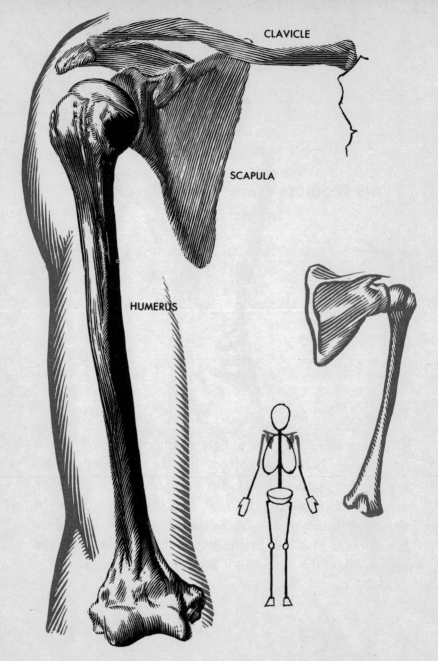

CLAVICLE

SCAPULA

HUMERUS

THE BONE OF THE UPPER ARM (Humerus)

The humerus hangs from the shoulder blade as a line hangs from a fishing pole. It is the largest bone in the upper body. From a front view, it resembles an elongated dumbbell: its wide head is shaped like a ball facing in toward the body, while its shaft narrows below the head and forms a graceful line to its base. There it fans out abruptly. At the very bottom of the humerus there is a formation that resembles a spool.

When the arm is held straight down, the shoulder blade and humerus look like a boy scout hatchet.

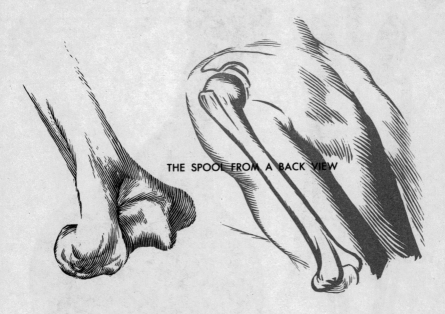

THE SPOOL FROM A BACK VIEW

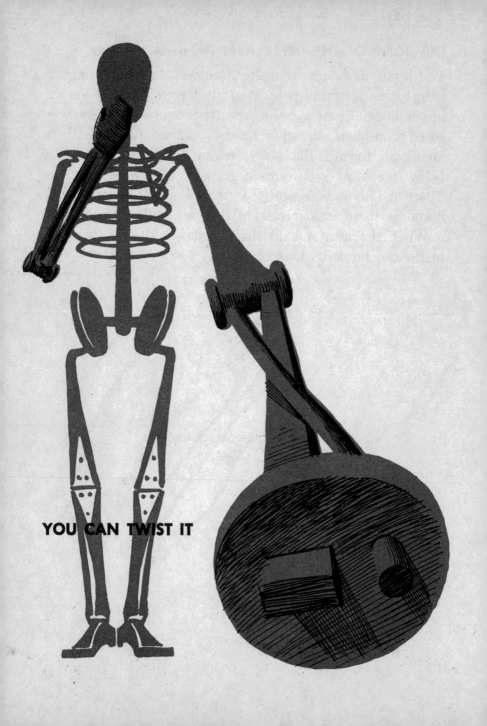

YOU CAN TWIST IT

AND BEND IT, AND TURN IT AROUND

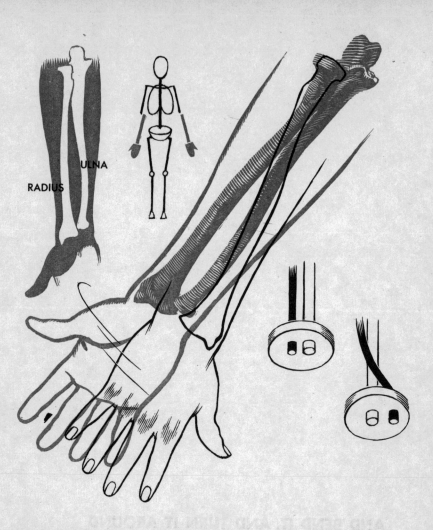

RADIUS

ULNA

THE BONES OF THE FOREARM
(Radius and Ulna)

Like the leg, the forearm consists of 2 bones running side by side. In the leg, the parallel bones allow the foot to turn slightly. In the arm, the parallel bones make it possible to turn the hand completely around.

The larger of the 2 bones in the forearm is the ulna. Its claw-shaped head is the widest part of this bone. The ulna tapers gracefully toward the bottom and runs from the elbow to the wrist, on the side of the little finger. On the thumb side, parallel with the ulna, is the radius. With the ulna, it forms the wrist and the elbow.

When the palm of the hand faces up, the ulna and radius are straight. The radius, by gliding over the ulna, makes it possible to turn the palm face down. A bone is too rigid to twist itself, but long, narrow bones, side by side, can roll over one another, giving flexible action to inflexible bones.

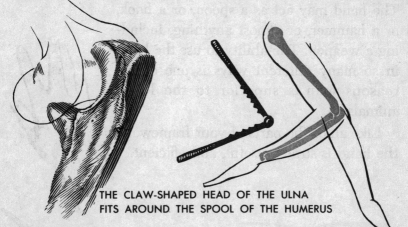

THE CLAW-SHAPED HEAD OF THE ULNA
FITS AROUND THE SPOOL OF THE HUMERUS

THE ELBOW

The elbow is formed by the spool at the base of the humerus that receives the claw at the head of the ulna. Like the knee, it is a hinge joint that locks when the arm is straight. The elbow makes the arm look and behave like a nutcracker.

THE HAND AND WRIST

The 8 bones of the wrist and the 19 bones of the palm and fingers make the hand the most useful tool in the world. The hand makes a hinge joint with the wrist and is able to move up and down, around and over. The thumb can reach around and touch any of the four fingers.

Each of the fingers has 3 joints; the thumb has 2. This makes the hand a flexible instrument, capable of great skill. The hand may act as a spoon, or a hook, or a hammer, or almost anything, including a weapon. The ability to use the hand in so many different ways is one of the reasons man is superior to the lower animals.

Like all of the parts of your framework, the hand is strong, useful, and efficient.

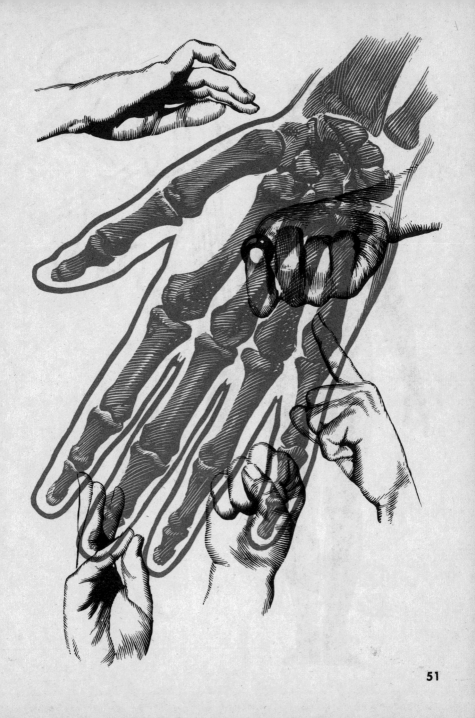

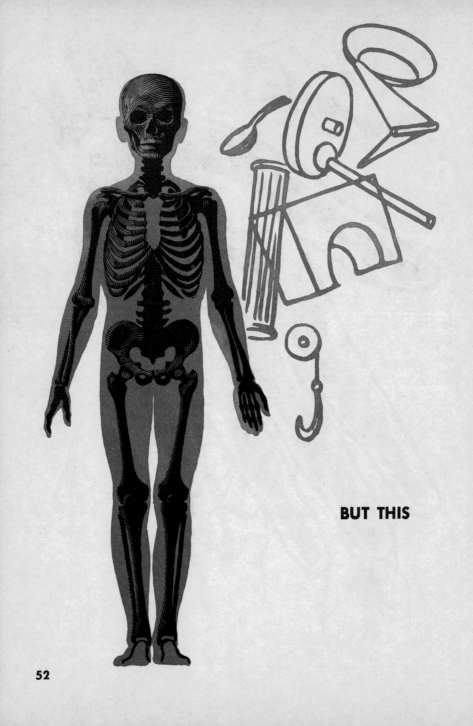

BUT THIS

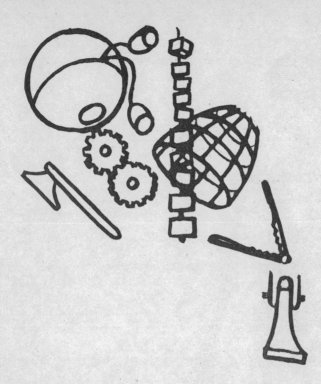

IS ONLY THE FRAMEWORK . . .

WHAT HOLDS US TOGETHER?   WHAT MAKES

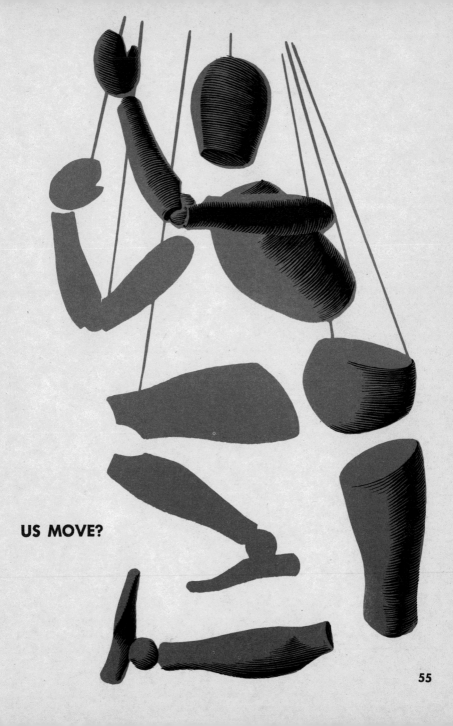

US MOVE?

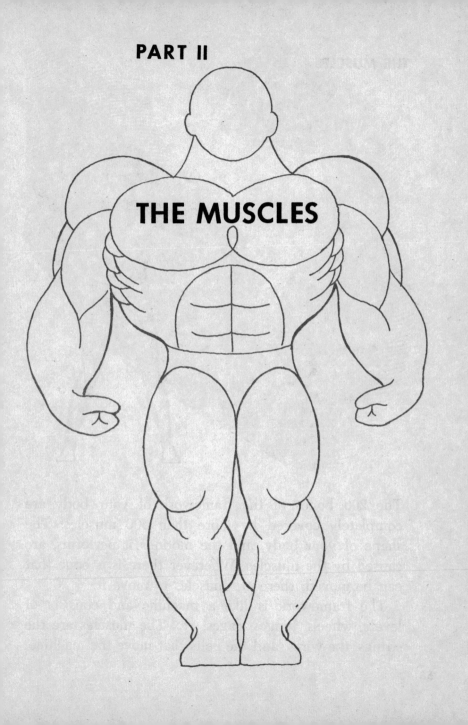

PART II

THE MUSCLES

THE MUSCLES

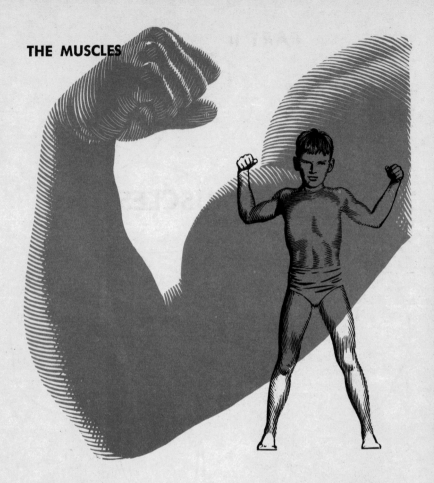

The 206 bones of the framework of your body are completely covered by more than 500 muscles. The shape of your body, and the motions it performs, are caused by the muscles. Wherever there is a bone that can be moved, there are muscles to move it.

The framework is like a machine and consists of levers, wheels, hinges, cages, etc. The muscles are the strings, the wires, and the belts that move the machine.

Muscles are made of many bundles of stringy fibers bound together in bunches. The main part of the muscle is fleshy and can contract and expand like a rubber band. Its ends, however, are of tough, stubborn tissue called tendon. By means of the tendon, the muscle is tightly bound to bone, skin, or other tissue. Each muscle is fixed at one point, and this is called its origin. The other end of the muscle is usually attached to that part of the body which it puts into action, and this is called its insertion. The ability of a muscle to contract toward its point of origin makes motion possible.

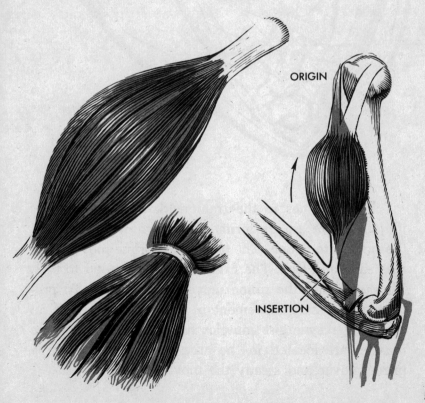

ORIGIN

INSERTION

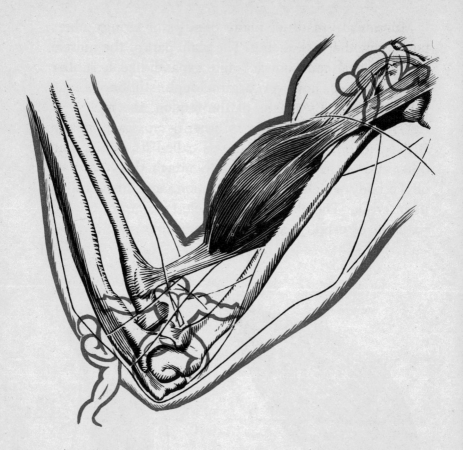

Like the bones in the framework, each muscle has its job. There are the prime movers, muscles that put the body into action. The origin of a prime mover must be steady and firm. The fixation muscles attend to that. They surround the prime mover at its origin. To prevent unnecessary movement in the performance of an action, the synergist muscles are called upon. These muscles are located in the area of the insertion of a prime mover and steady the moving joints.

Each muscle in the body has an opponent in the same area. For every muscle that bends a joint there is one that straightens it. Similarly, for every muscle that raises a bone there is one that lowers it. In the arm the muscle called the biceps contracts, the triceps relaxes, and the arm is bent. When the triceps contracts, the biceps relaxes, and the arm returns to its original position. This harmony occurs all over the body.

The muscles can, and do, change their shapes when they are active. When a muscle is at rest it never completely relaxes, and though we may be motionless, our muscles are always alert. This is what is meant by muscle tone. Without muscle tone the jaw would sag, the eyelids would droop, and breathing would stop.

Muscles move us and keep us alive.

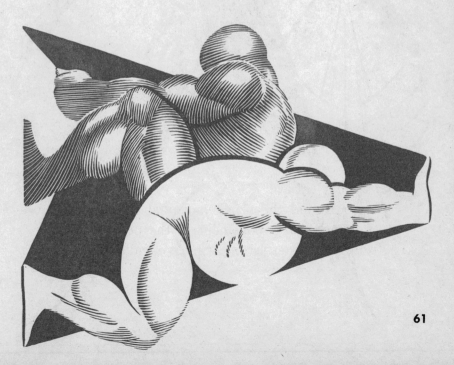

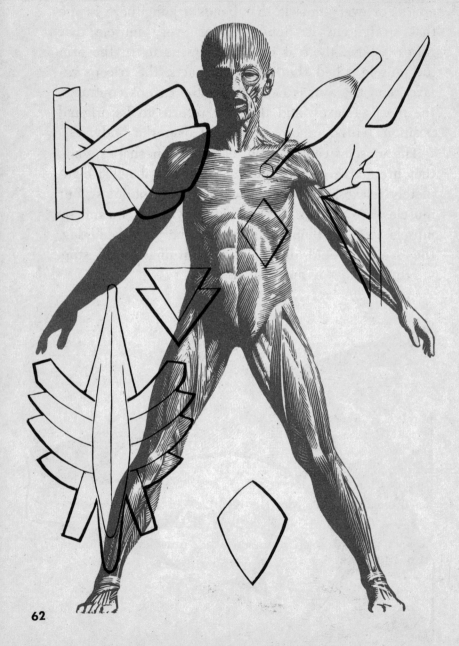

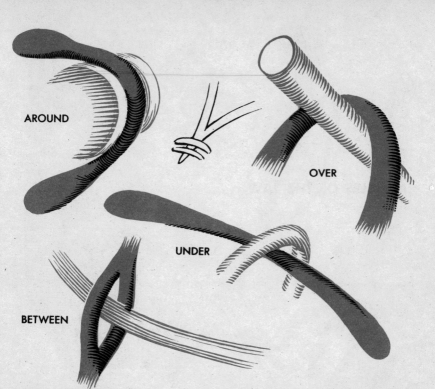

AROUND

OVER

UNDER

BETWEEN

The human body is a three-dimensional jigsaw puzzle, in which each piece fits in with the others perfectly, and is neither too large nor too small to do the job it does. Although the muscles are all bunched together, no one muscle interferes with the work of another.

Flat-shaped, round-shaped, long, thin, and diamond-shaped, the muscles cover the body. There are muscles that twist upon themselves. There are muscles that overlap each other like the shingles of a house. Some muscles go around bones, others go over bones. Many muscles are squeezed between other muscles and bones. In spite of all this crowding, we are so well organized that the result is one of beauty and harmony.

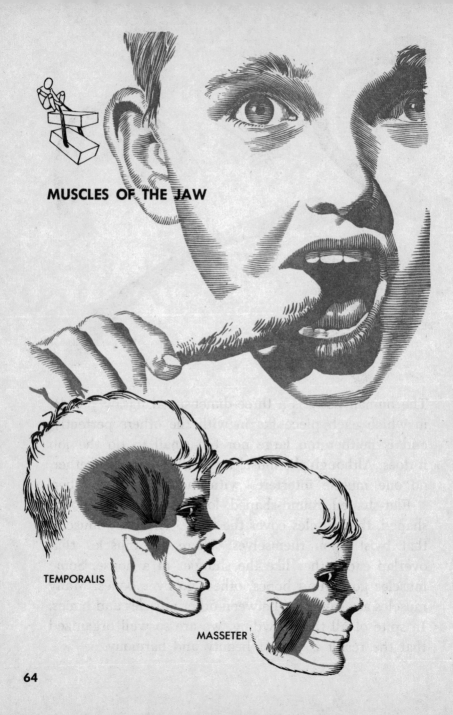

MUSCLES OF THE JAW

TEMPORALIS

MASSETER

Powerful muscles hold the movable lower jaw to the immovable bones of the head and provide the power needed to bite and chew. Like the chains on a drawbridge, these muscles raise the lower jaw.

The muscles that lift the jaw are the temporalis and masseter muscles. The temporalis has its origin at the cranium on the side of the head. This muscle is wide at the top and narrows down to a point as it goes under the cheekbone. Its point is inserted on the lower jaw. The masseter that helps to raise the lower jaw is also at the side of the head, but it has its origin at the cheekbone, and its insertion—a wide one—at the lower jaw.

Attached to the bottom of the jaw are the muscles that lower the jaw. They are not as strong as the muscles that raise it. When you open your mouth, you do it either to utter sounds or to make room for food—actions which do not require much effort. But the teeth of the upper and lower jaws must grind food. The upper jaw remains motionless; the lower jaw does all the work. That is why you have a set of strong muscles to raise the lower jaw.

MUSCLES OF EXPRESSION

The muscles of the face are honest. When we try to hide what is in our minds, the muscles of the face give us away. As we grow older we try to control them. And even then, it is hard to laugh when our hearts tell us to cry.

The muscles of the face are small and thin and are scattered all over the face. Their origin is in the bones of the head and their insertion into the flesh of the face. The muscles of the face are hidden by a thin layer of fat. They become pronounced only when we make faces or frown. Without these muscles, communication would be more difficult. Our facial expressions, very often, are more eloquent than words. Lower animals are incapable of expressing emotions because they do not have as many facial muscles as we have.

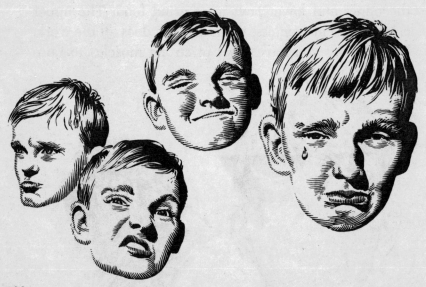

68

MUSCLES OF THE NECK

One fourth of all your muscles are in the face and neck. To describe each muscle would need more space than we can take here. So we will concern ourselves with only those muscles that perform the main actions of the body and are responsible for its shape.

Two of the more important muscles that move the head, the sternomastoid muscles, originate behind the ears at the base of the skull. Resembling two rubber hoses that bulge in the center, these muscles run down each side of the neck and meet at its base. They, with the aid of other neck muscles that originate in the back, enable you to turn, bend, lower, and raise the head.

To see and hear you must be able to turn the head in all directions. Your safety depends a great deal on the ability of the neck to turn the head quickly and easily.

MUSCLES OF THE SHOULDER AND BREAST

In order to raise an arm, a great deal of muscular force is needed. The muscle that does most of the work is the one that bulges at the shoulder. The shoulder muscle is shaped like a triangular shield, and is named the deltoid, because it resembles the Greek letter Delta. Attached to the outer side of the collarbone and shoulder blade, the shoulder muscle is inserted near the top of the bone of the upper arm. This muscle raises the arm and thrusts it forward and backward.

The shoulder muscle gets quite a bit of help from the breast muscle, or pectoralis major, which consists of many flat bands. These bands spread from the collar-bone down the outside of the breastbone and across the seventh rib. The outer ends of the muscular bands over-lap, twist upon themselves, and are inserted to the top inner side of the bone of the upper arm. When the arm is raised the muscle untwists. The shoulder muscle lifts the arm; the breast muscle lowers it. The raising and lowering of any part of the body are separate actions. A muscle that lifts a body member does only that. To return the member to its original position, a different muscle is required.

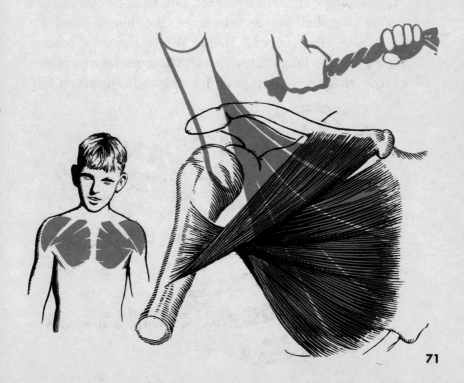

THE RIB MUSCLES

Working continuously, like two engines, the muscles of the ribs raise and lower the rib cage so that we may breathe. These muscles are called the intercostal muscles, and fill the space between the ribs.

The external intercostal muscles raise the rib cage, each muscle raising the rib below it. The internal intercostal muscles lower or depress the ribs by pulling down the ribs above.

Other muscles that help pull the rib cage down come up from the hipbone and clutch the rib cage from the front and side, pulling it down.

When the ribs are raised and lowered by the rib muscles, the lungs are squeezed and then released. Like the rubber ball on an atomizer, the lungs expel air when the ribs squeeze them. When the ribs release their grip, the lungs draw in air. The muscles and bones of the ribs were designed for this all-important job.

EXTERNAL
INTERCOSTAL MUSCLES

INTERNAL
INTERCOSTAL MUSCLES

THE TRUNK

The trunk is that part of the body which extends from the shoulders to the hips. The muscles of the trunk cover and protect us as bark covers and protects a tree.

In the trunk are located the roots of the muscles that move the head, the arms, the legs, and, of course, the trunk itself. The largest muscles in the body are located in the back. These muscles hold the spine straight and provide you with great power. In the front of your trunk is a wall of muscle. This wall is a flexible coat of armor that protects the digestive organs. The job of bending you forward and backward is assigned to the muscles in the front of your body. When these muscles are in tune, you look trim and fit.

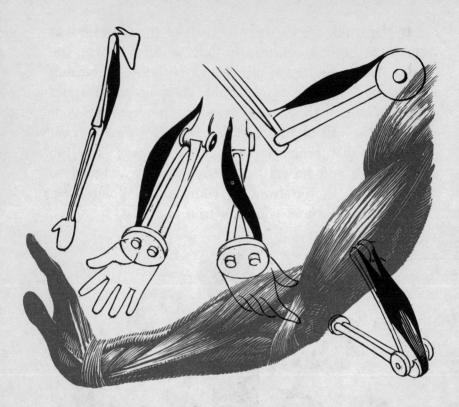

MUSCLES OF THE ARM AND LEG

The long and wiry muscles of the arms and legs (similar to the strings that move a puppet) are concerned with only one thing—movement. These muscles do not protect any vital organs. They are attached to bones that were designed to move in many ways.

The muscles of the upper arm bend the arm by raising the forearm. These same muscles also assist in turning the arm. The muscles of the forearm move and turn the hand.

The muscles in the thigh move the lower leg, and the muscles in the lower leg move the foot. As in the arm, each section of the leg is controlled by a group of inserted muscles that originate in the section above it.

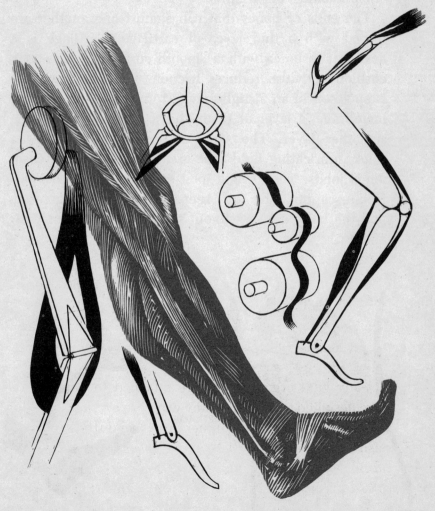

LUBRICATION

Motion is created by the muscles moving the bones. When the bones move, they rub against one another. To run smoothly, a machine that has moving parts must be oiled regularly. The human machine, unlike any other machine, oils itself.

The ends of bones that rub against one another are tipped with a thin layer of cartilage. Cartilage is a flexible substance with a smooth surface. It acts as a cushion and also reduces friction. Each moving joint is enclosed in an airtight cavity formed by the synovial membrane, a layer of tissue that is lined with an even smoother layer. The synovial membrane produces a thick, lubricating fluid that greases the cartilage-cushioned joints. The airtight joint cavity prevents the "oil" from escaping. The "oil" keeps the joints well greased, and the body moves without squeaks, stiffness, or wear and tear.

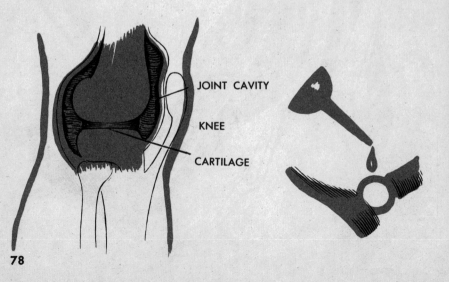

JOINT CAVITY

KNEE

CARTILAGE

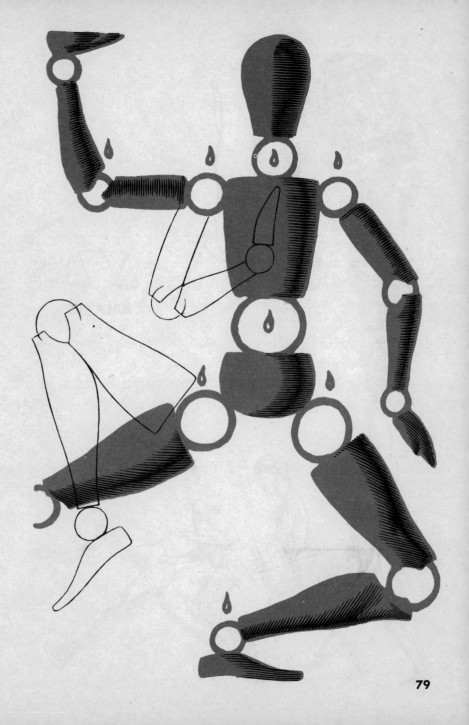

BALANCE

Walking seems like a very simple action. But walking would be impossible without the cooperation of every muscle in your body. The act of walking is the result of the body's harmony and balance.

With every step we take, about 300 muscles are in motion. When the left leg goes forward, the right arm comes out to balance it. The shoulders swing to the left, the hips to the right. The left foot touches the ground, and the left leg pulls us forward. Then the right leg reaches out, and every muscle that was tense now relaxes while their mates, that were relaxed, become tense. And so you walk. The principle of balance and counterbalance that takes place inside your bodies is carried out in all your actions. When you are clumsy or awkward it means only that you have violated the laws of the body.

**MUSCLES AND BONES ARE VERY PRETTY
BUT NOT VERY SMART. THEY STILL**

NEED SOMETHING TO TELL THEM WHAT TO DO—

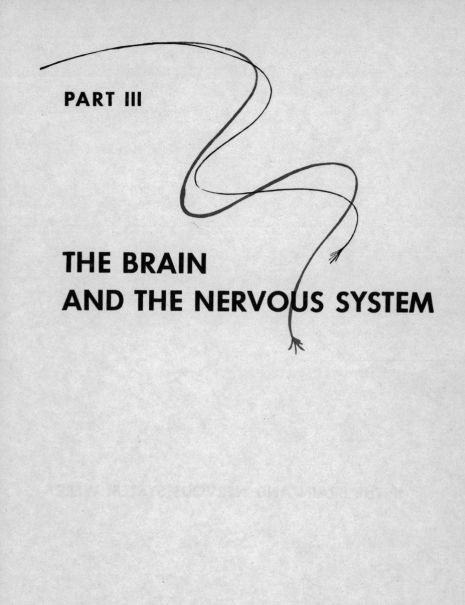

PART III

THE BRAIN
AND THE NERVOUS SYSTEM

IF THE BRAIN AND NERVOUS SYSTEM WERE

MADE OF FAMILIAR OBJECTS—
YOU WOULD LOOK LIKE
MEN FROM MARS

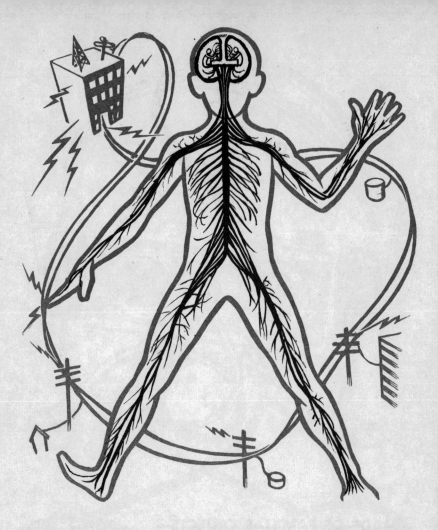

THE CENTRAL NERVOUS SYSTEM

The central nervous system consists of the brain, the spinal cord, and the nerves that extend from the spinal cord. As a simple illustration, the central nervous system might be compared to an electrical communication station. The brain is like a switchboard, receiving and answering messages continuously. The spinal cord is the main cable through which incoming and outgoing messages flow. And the nerves are the wires that run from the main cable to the remote corners of the body, leaving no area without a signaling device. The incoming messages are carried on a network made up of the sensory nerves. The answers are delivered by way of a companion network composed of the motor nerves.

All living tissue is composed of tiny, microscopic bits of matter, or cells. The cells that make up the nervous system are called neurons. All cells react to stimulation, but none in the unusual way that neurons do. Unlike any other cell, the neuron is capable of transmitting an impulse to its neighbor. The billions of neurons packed together into the nerve paths deliver a message to the brain in the following way.

The impulse travels rapidly in one direction, each neuron disturbing the next one along the route of a sensory nerve until the section of the central office that takes care of such matters is informed. The reply is flashed back in the identical manner through a motor nerve to the muscle it activates. The first neuron in a sensory nerve that is stimulated starts a chain reaction that ends with the contraction of a muscle through a motor nerve.

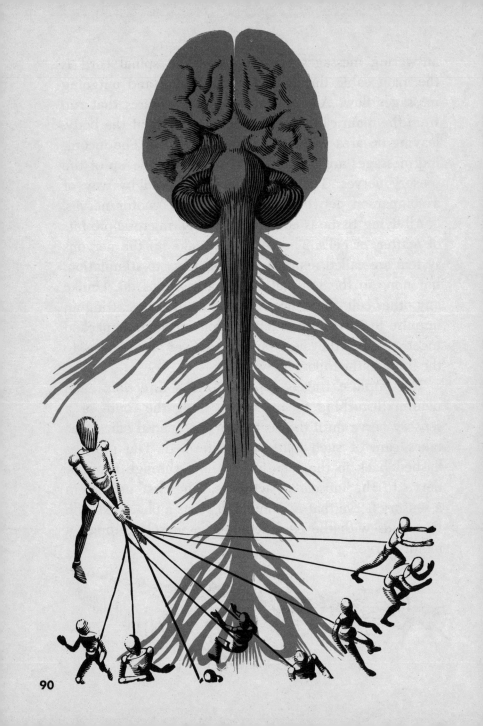

THE BRAIN AND THE SPINAL CORD

The brain is in complete charge of the vast, complex operation just described. It occupies the entire top floor of the skull, and from this lofty fortress it guides and controls you. The brain organizes the scattered parts of your body into one unit, makes you aware of things, and incites you to action. The brain also runs the internal machinery of your body without bothering you about it, so that you may devote your time to the things you want to do.

Almost all the sensory and motor nerves that activate the muscles extend from the spinal cord. The cord is a long cable-like structure made up of hundreds of nerve fibers. It is suspended in the bony canal formed by the long string of vertebrae, bathed by a clear liquid called the spinal fluid. The cord runs up the spine and through the opening at the bottom of the cranium, where it expands and becomes the brain. The brain itself is divided into three sections: the medulla, the cerebellum, and the cerebrum.

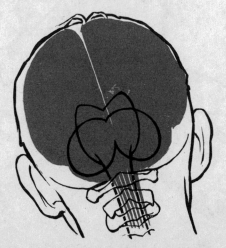

The enlargement of the spinal cord just inside the skull, at the bottom of the brain, is the medulla. The medulla is the busiest section of the brain. All messages received by the brain must pass through the medulla—consequently all of the answers must pass through the medulla on their way back.

Above and behind the medulla is the cerebellum. It is about the size of a small handball. The cerebellum makes it possible for you to walk, dance, play games, or do anything that requires coordination and balance.

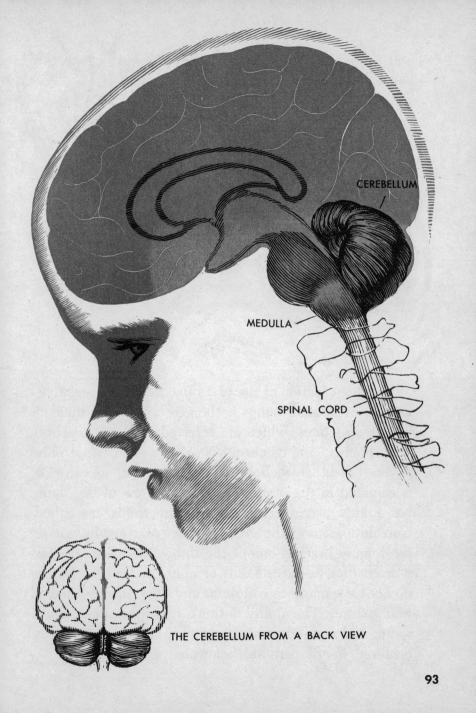

CEREBELLUM

MEDULLA

SPINAL CORD

THE CEREBELLUM FROM A BACK VIEW

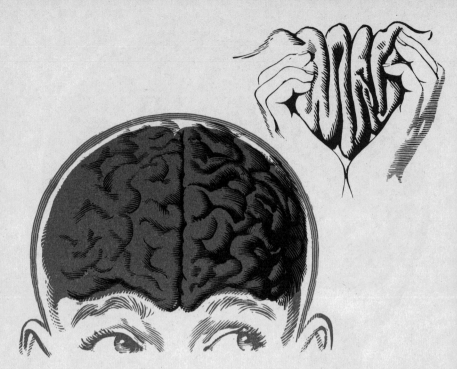

The giant section of the brain that makes us sensitive, intelligent human beings is the cerebrum. It is divided into two sections, which are referred to as the cerebral hemispheres. The cerebrum is so large that it not only covers the other sections of the brain but, because it is confined in the limited and rigid hollow of the skull, has folded over on itself. The many folds are called convolutions, and the great number of convolutions in the human brain is one of the things that distinguishes it from that in lower forms of animals. Lower animals do not have many convolutions and, therefore, not much brain matter. The ability to think, remember, see, speak, write, and make decisions involving voluntary action is centered in the cerebral hemispheres.

The brain keeps in touch with the world around us through its agents, the senses.

The eye is the camera of the brain. It tells the brain what things look like and where to find them. Odors sent to the brain by way of the nose tell the brain what things are. Taste tells us whether food is good or bad. Vibrations become sounds to the brain when they pass through the tunnel of the ear. When heat, cold, pain, or pressure touches any part of our body the skin informs the brain. The sense of touch, or feeling, is located all over the surface of the body.

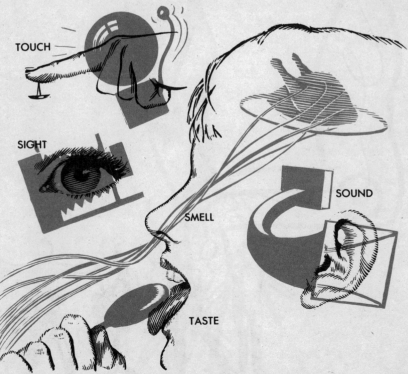

TOUCH

SIGHT

SMELL

SOUND

TASTE

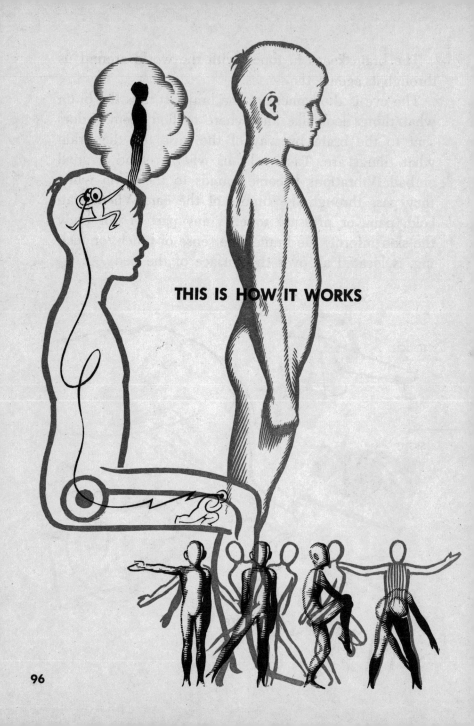

THIS IS HOW IT WORKS

VOLUNTARY ACTION

The brain must be excited into action. We do not rise from a sitting position without a reason. Whether the reason is important or not matters little to the brain. All voluntary messages are of equal importance. They must be obeyed. The message to stand up may reach the brain through one of the senses. The brain answers through the motor nerves. It knows which of these nerves control the muscles that move the bones that can make you rise. When you give the order the standing muscles are contracted, the sitting muscles relaxed. The gears turn, the hinges lock, the pulleys pull. You are standing up.

If you have performed an action many times, the brain has a record of this action in its vast files. Standing and sitting are actions that you perform constantly, so the brain, in a fraction of a second, gets the picture out of the file, remembers exactly how it was done, and starts the action which will end in your standing up, although it may be doing a dozen other things at the same time. That is why it is possible to play games in which many actions are performed at once.

WARNING SIGNALS

REFLEX ACTION

Some messages that the sensory nerves send to the brain are marked *urgent*. They are the messages of pain. All over the surface of your body are sensory nerves on the lookout for anything that might hurt you. When the point of a pin pricks your finger, for example, the nerve that carries the message of pain to the brain does not wait to see if the brain is busy doing anything else. It demands that the message be answered—immediately. The call for help is answered by way of the motor nerves, and the muscles of the hand snap the finger away from the pin.

These actions are not planned, nor do we have to learn how to do them. They are called reflex actions. Most reflex actions are the result of an excited sensory nerve calling a motor nerve to its aid. In many cases the message goes no farther than the spinal cord, where the connection between sensory and motor nerves takes place. Other reflex actions happen through the brain. Bright light, unexpected noises, and odors reach the brain through one of the five senses, and you blink, jump, or bring some other motor response into play.

The reflex mechanism of the brain and spinal cord is alert even when you are asleep. It is always protecting and warning you.

THE BRAIN MAKES IT FUN TO BE ALIVE

The ability of the brain to store information, become excited, adapt itself, and make decisions explains why you can walk, talk, and use your body. Sometimes an action is done once, and the brain remembers how to do it. At other times an act must be done over and over before the brain makes a record and puts it in the files. If a new action includes some old ones, the brain sorts out those actions that are familiar and concentrates on that part of the action it must learn. Actions that are repeated often become habits. You do many things at the same time without planning how they should be done.

You decide to watch television, for example. Without the cerebrum—the thinking part of your brain—you could never make this decision. Without eyes and ears to see and hear, you could not even imagine what television is. The sense of taste gives you the nice idea of eating some candy while you are watching. Your sensory nerves tell you that your dog is soft and warm, and the motor nerves enable you to sit and hold the dog, to turn the knob of your set, and to put the candy in your mouth and chew it. All these acts would be impossible without the central nervous system. The ability of the brain to keep these actions apart yet do them all at the same time makes being alive fun.

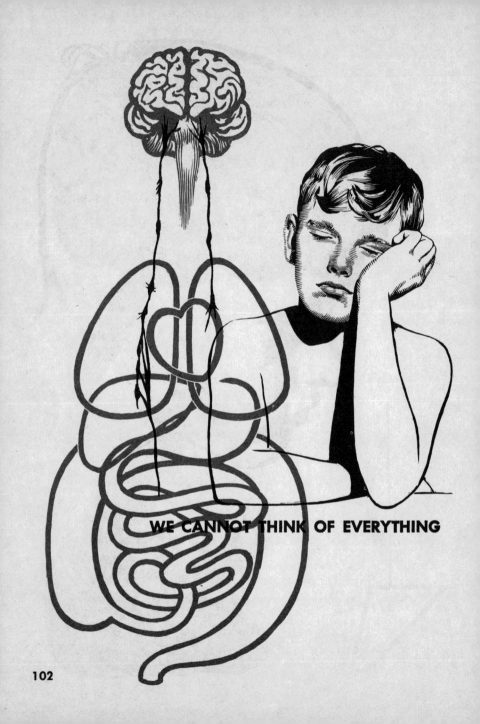

WE CANNOT THINK OF EVERYTHING

THE SYMPATHETIC NERVES

The sympathetic nervous system originates outside the medulla. Descending on either side of the spinal cord, it leads to the vital organs. The sympathetic nerves make the heart beat and the lungs breathe, and direct the movements of all the vital organs. These nerves work whether we like it or not. We have no control over them. They need no one to tell them what to do. Since the day we were born, they have been thinking for themselves. We did not have to teach the lungs how to give us air. The heart knew how to beat from the very beginning. While it lets us control most of our outside actions, the brain very wisely tells us "please don't bother" where such important internal affairs are concerned. After all, we are only human, and we may forget to tell the heart to pump a little faster when we're chasing an infield hit. This would be a great pity!

The job of the nervous system is to activate or excite muscle. The sympathetic nerves do this with miraculous skill. All your vital and internal organs have layers of muscle of one form or another. The action of a muscle is one of contraction. And every function that the internal organs perform is produced by the continuous contracting and relaxing of muscles. Only the rhythm varies: the timing of the lungs, the heart, or the intestine is different, and the tempo of each of these organs changes under different conditions.

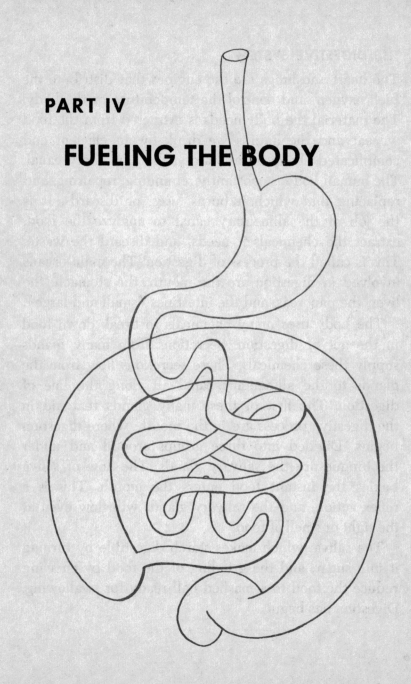

PART IV

FUELING THE BODY

THE DIGESTIVE SYSTEM

The heart and lungs are the engines that distribute the fuel, oxygen, and control the temperature of the body. The material the body needs is extracted from the food we eat and the liquids we drink by an efficient and complicated chemical laboratory, the alimentary canal. The human body is constantly rebuilding, repairing, and replacing that which it burns, uses, or discards. It is the job of the alimentary canal to analyze the food, extract the chemicals it needs, and discard the waste. This is called the process of digestion. The main organs involved in digestion are the mouth, the stomach, the liver, the pancreas, and the intestines (small and large).

The body uses many chemicals to break down food in the act of digestion. Secretions from many glands supply these chemicals. These secretions flow from the glands to the alimentary canal all along the line of digestion. The first of these many glands that aid in the digestive process are in the mouth, where digestion begins. Divided into three groups around and under the tongue are the salivary glands. The flow of saliva begins the instant food enters the mouth. This is a reflex action, and the salivary glands will flow even at the sight or smell of food.

The saliva, which makes starch digestible by turning it into sugar, and the grinding of the food by chewing reduce the food to a mashed ball ready for swallowing. Digestion has begun.

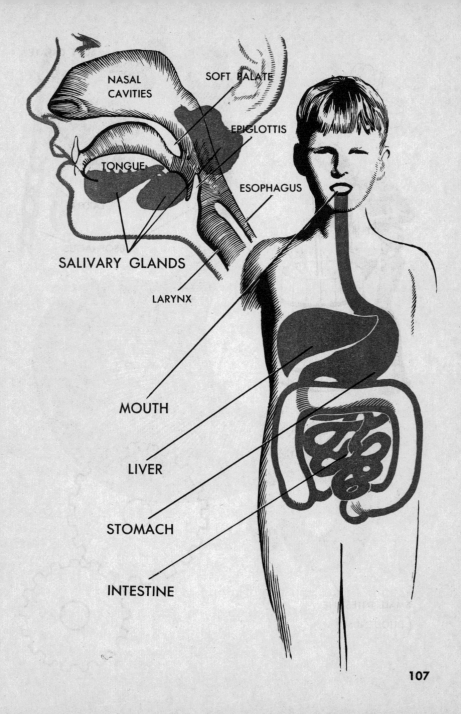

NASAL CAVITIES

SOFT PALATE

EPIGLOTTIS

TONGUE

ESOPHAGUS

SALIVARY GLANDS

LARYNX

MOUTH

LIVER

STOMACH

INTESTINE

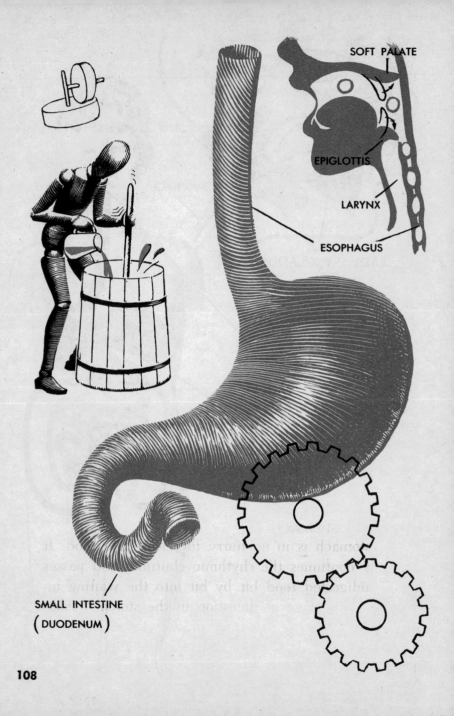

SOFT PALATE

EPIGLOTTIS

LARYNX

ESOPHAGUS

SMALL INTESTINE
(DUODENUM)

THE STOMACH

The food is swallowed. This appears to be a simple process, yet it is one of the most complicated muscular reflexes the body is called upon to perform. The esophagus, or tube leading to the stomach, the larynx, or pipe leading to the lungs, and the back of the nose are all in the same area of the mouth.

At the moment of swallowing, the soft palate is drawn upward to shut off the nasal cavities, to prevent choking. At the same time a flap of cartilage which projects backward at the base of the tongue covers the larynx, and allows the food to slide over it. The esophagus takes the food and forces it toward the stomach. The food does not drop into the stomach; it is carried systematically down the esophagus toward the stomach by a series of muscular movements, called peristalsis.

Now in the stomach the food receives the same treatment it received in the mouth. The mashing continues. The powerful muscles of the stomach grind and churn the food, while the stomach secretes digestive juices more powerful than saliva. The starch in food is made digestible by the saliva. The gastric juices make proteins digestible.

The stomach is in no hurry to release the food. It patiently continues the rhythmic churning and passes the semidigested food bit by bit into the waiting intestines. This stage of digestion in the stomach takes three to four hours, depending on the amount we have eaten. Otherwise we would be continuously hungry.

THE INTESTINE

The final stage of digestion takes place in the intestine, where the food, mashed in the mouth and further broken down in the stomach, is carefully taken apart and distributed by the blood throughout the body.

The intestine is actually a long tube five or six times the length of your body. Like the brain, it forms convolutions, so that it can fit into the abdominal area of the body. The intestine starts at the lower opening of the stomach. Like the stomach, the intestine is lined with muscles that contract and expand continuously. The semidigested food it has received from the stomach begins its last, long journey.

The first ten or twelve inches of the intestine are called the duodenum. Secretions flow from its walls, and it is in the area of the duodenum that bile from the liver and pancreatic juice from the pancreas are received. The food continues to be moved forward in conveyer-belt style.

All along the trip chemicals are extracted from the food and immediately shipped along the vast network of the body's waterways—the arteries—to the waiting and hungry tissues of the body.

By the time the food has traveled through some 20 feet of intestine it is almost a liquid. All the valuable chemicals that the body could use have been absorbed.

The remains of the digested food now enter the last part of the intestine, the colon. The first four fifths of the intestine is called the small intestine. The colon is known as the large intestine. Much wider in diameter than the small intestine, it passes up the right side of the abdomen, makes a sharp bend across to the left side of the abdomen, and down the left side, forming a three-sided frame for the small intestine.

What remains of the completely digested food is waste and is passed out of the body through the colon, and through the rectum, which is the very last part of the large intestine.

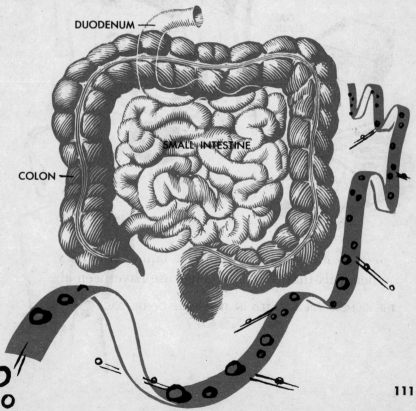

DUODENUM

SMALL INTESTINE

COLON

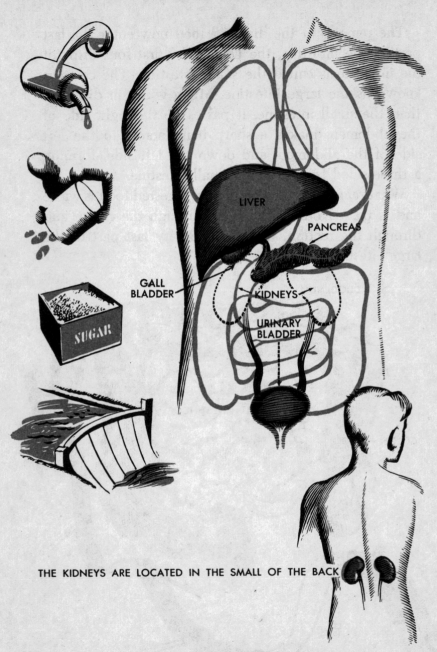

LIVER

PANCREAS

GALL
BLADDER

KIDNEYS

URINARY
BLADDER

SUGAR

THE KIDNEYS ARE LOCATED IN THE SMALL OF THE BACK

THE LIVER AND KIDNEYS

Glands play a very important part in the process of digestion. The largest of these glands is the liver. The liver serves the body as perhaps no other organ does. It aids digestion by producing a secretion called bile, which is stored in a small sac called the gall bladder. The work of breaking down the food (started in the mouth and the stomach) continues in the intestine, with the help of the bile and juices formed by another gland, the pancreas. Both the bile and the pancreatic juice flow into the duodenum by way of a common tube.

The liver also keeps a close watch on the blood stream. It rids the blood of many harmful products it may absorb from the alimentary canal during the process of digestion. Any excess sugar produced by the body is stored for future use by the liver. And the liver, by retaining any excess blood that may flood the heart, watches your precious heart to see that it is not overloaded.

Harmful products from food are sent by way of the blood stream to the kidneys. Water, salts, and protein waste are separated from the blood by the kidneys through cells arranged like a filter to perform this job. The harmful products are poured by means of a tube into a reservoir called the bladder, which in turn is emptied through another tube, the urethra, leading out of the body.

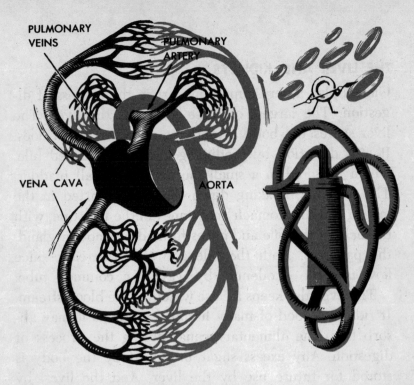

PULMONARY VEINS

PULMONARY ARTERY

VENA CAVA

AORTA

THE HEART AND BLOOD STREAM

The heart is the pump that forces a heated liquid called blood throughout your entire body. The blood consists of millions and millions of tiny round red and white cells, or corpuscles, floating in a serum. The red corpuscles carry the oxygen from the lungs to tissues and cells throughout the body. For every 5000 red corpuscles, there are 8 white ones. The white corpuscles are the soldiers of the body. Their duty is to protect us from invading microbes. No army could compare with the bravery of this white-corpuscle army. They attack and destroy any and all enemies that dare to invade the blood stream. It is a fight to the death, and victory demands its price. The white corpuscles that fall in battle take the form of "matter," or pus.

The blood goes to the lungs for oxygen—an important gas, needed by the body to sustain life—and to the intestines to pick up the digested food and carry it to all parts of the body. The pipes that carry the blood are the arteries, veins, and the capillaries. Of these, the arteries are the pipes that feed the body.

The blood goes from the heart to the lungs by way of the pulmonary artery. The pulmonary artery has many branches, and these branches, in turn, have many smaller branches of their own. The tiniest and most numerous of these branches are called the capillaries. The blood gets the oxygen from the lungs by absorbing it through the thin walls of the capillaries. The lung capillaries then unite to form the pulmonary veins that return the oxygen-loaded blood to the heart. This blood then passes to the main artery, the aorta, on the left side of the heart. It is through the many branches and capillaries of the main artery that oxygen from the lungs and vital substances from the intestines are carried to every organ, muscle, and nerve in your body.

By the time the blood reaches the ends of the capillaries it has collected a good deal of waste matter, primarily carbon dioxide. At this point, the capillaries run into tiny veins that become bigger as they approach the heart. The largest veins combine and form the great vein, or vena cava, that flows into the right side of the heart. It is by way of the veins, then, that the blood is returned to the heart and sent back again through the arteries. Ordinarily, each trip takes 23 seconds.

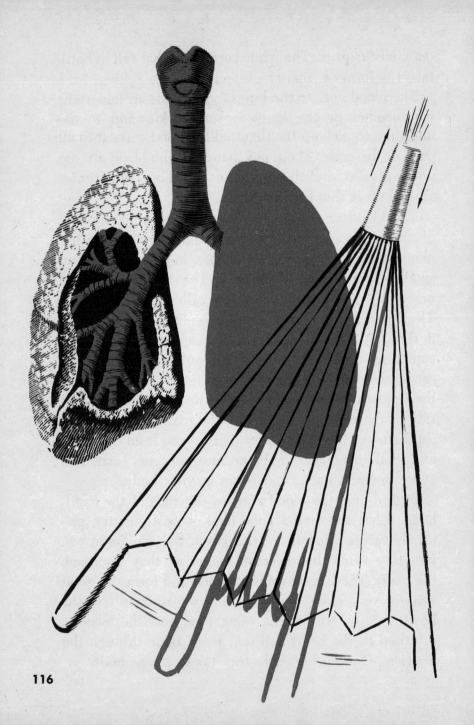

THE LUNGS

Since the moment you took your first breath, your lungs have never been without air. The ribs and their muscles, by expanding and contracting, make the lungs act like a bellows. When a bellows expands, a partial vacuum is created inside. Air rushes in to fill the vacuum. When the bellows is pressed together, the air is forced out. This is the way the lungs work. When the lungs are expanded, they are full of air. The blood takes the oxygen from the air and leaves the waste gas, carbon dioxide, in the lungs. The carbon dioxide is squeezed out of the lungs as the ribs contract.

Oxygen is used to create heat, and your body cannot work unless it has heat. Since it is an engine that operates at a temperature of about 98 degrees, the body needs a lot of oxygen. The lungs supply it.

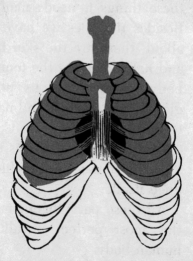

YOUR BODY IS A MACHINE

that does a multitude of things. To do these things it needs many, many parts. Besides the ones we have already talked about, there are the skin that covers you and helps regulate the temperature of the body by means of its pores and sweat glands, and the hair and nails, which help to make you attractive.

And the miracle of this machine is that it carries the seed with which it can reproduce itself.

All these parts together are what make this most perfect of all machines—the human body.

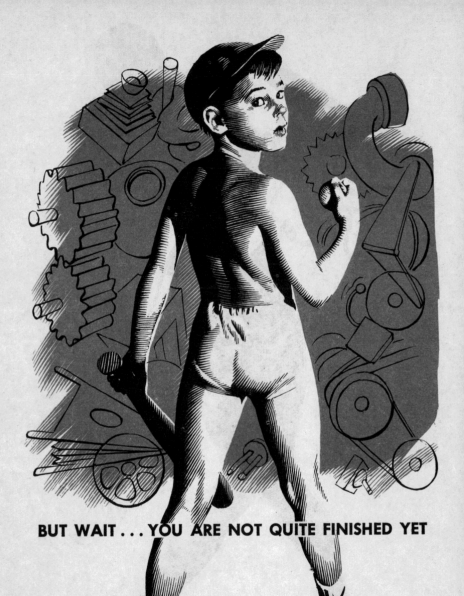

BUT WAIT...YOU ARE NOT QUITE FINISHED YET

THIS IS JUST THE MACHINERY...

WE ARE MORE THAN JUST MACHINES

BECAUSE WE LOVE AND WANT TO BE LOVED

. . . AND HAVE PITY

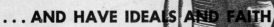

...AND KNOW WHY

...AND DREAM

...AND HAVE IDEALS AND FAITH

THESE GIFTS OF THE SPIRIT

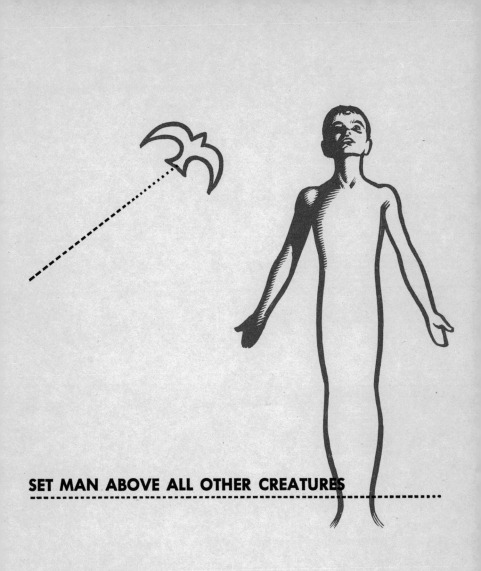

SET MAN ABOVE ALL OTHER CREATURES